The Mystery of
Marriage

The Mystery of
Marriage

by
Isaac D. Martin

Rod and Staff Publishers, Inc.
P.O. Box 3, Hwy. 172
Crockett, Kentucky 41413
Telephone: (606) 522-4348

Printed in U.S.A

ISBN 978-07399-2327-6

Catalog no. 2568

5   6   7   8   9   —   24   23   22   21   20   19   18   17   16   15

Table of Contents

Introduction 11

1. The Wonder 17

2. The Plan 26

3. The Wife...34

4. The Husband 41

5. The Union 45

6. The Complexity..57

7. The Secret 61

8. Heirs Together 64

Introduction

"This is a great mystery," wrote the apostle Paul in Ephesians 5:32. Was he speaking about human marriage or about the relationship of Christ to the church?

Looking at the context, we see that Paul was speaking about both. Marriage carries mystery, just as the relationship of Christ to His church does. In this book we will focus on marriage.

When my wife and I married, we thought we knew each other quite well. Thankfully God did not show us immediately how ignorant we were. As we settled down to the real business of living together and blending together, we discovered that we needed God's help very much.

As we walked with the Lord, He helped us through every difficulty. He magnified Himself to us by showing us a right way through each trial. We marveled over the years as the mystery of marriage unfolded to us. As we focused on the designer of our marriage, the "kaleidoscope" of mystery yielded beauty and delight.

The mystery stretches beyond man's ability to

comprehend or explain. The exclusive interchange between a masculine and a feminine character makes it a mystery that only God could have designed. The more a couple stays focused on God, the greater will be their wonder at all God had in mind when He designed marriage, and the greater will be their blessings.

The intricacy of marriage adds to its mystery. *Intricate* means "entangled or involved, having many interrelated parts or facets; something complicated and hard to be understood." After more than forty years, I am still awed by the mystery of marriage—the intricate design that God has woven into the fabric of this relationship.

God writes infinity into every Biblical union. We should not expect to discover everything about it in a year or two. We can spend a lifetime discovering the infinite and intricate wisdom of God's design for our marriage.

God created the universe, but He did not tell us how He designed its interrelationships. He did give man the interest and the intelligence to discover the movement of the earth in relation to the planets and stars. Those who study the stars and planets can show you how it all works together. They have been able to make planetariums that illustrate the interrelationships of the heavenly universe. You can also get printed guides to tell you where each star or planet is on any day of the year.

God also created plants, each with its distinguishing characteristics. The botanist can revel for hours, studying the features of a certain plant. Considering the myriads of plants scattered over the earth, he can spend a lifetime studying plants. The animal kingdom and the sea world also intrigue those who dedicate their lives to their study. God's infinity is written in all that He does. Blessed are they who believe that God created the universe and who allow themselves to marvel and worship their Creator.

God also created humans. Genesis gives us a few more details about this than about other parts of Creation. God created a man who needed a helper. The woman was a special creation designed especially for man. The Bible tells how God took a rib from man and made a woman. He then brought the woman to Adam, and Adam decided that she should be called woman because she was taken out of man. Then the Bible says, "Therefore shall a man leave his father and his mother, and shall cleave unto his wife: and they shall be one flesh" (Genesis 2:24). The apostle Paul quotes this verse in Ephesians 5:31, adding in verse 32, "This is a great mystery."

The mystery of marriage can not be subject to scientific investigation or to laboratory experimentation. It serves to keep the marriage relationship a continual marvel as the husband and wife together discover God's intricate design in their marriage. It causes them to worship the infinitely wise Creator. It keeps the union rewarding and appealing until death.

Since man has subjected marriage to investigation and experimentation, its sacredness has largely disappeared in the world. Many couples are unfaithful to each other, and many more are dissatisfied with each other. The world tries to educate children and youth on all they should know for passionate relationships, yet divorce rates escalate. The effect is the same as when scientists study the created works of God without believing in God. When they reduce everything to a mere material existence, they have robbed the world of its glory. Likewise, when they study marriage as merely a physical experience, they have no way of seeing the infinite design God created in marriage.

Investigators have discovered that married couples benefit in ways that live-in partners never realize. Live-in partners face some of the stresses of marriage without the security of marriage and are no better off emotionally than if they lived alone. Married couples experience much less difficulty in these areas. Unbelievers cannot fully explain this, and children of God do not need to. Ah, the mystery and wonder that God tied up in marriage!

This book is an attempt to bring our minds back to the Creator. If every married couple believed that God has a unique design for their particular marriage, they would set out to discover what that is. This would free them from the bondage of statistics, free them from trying to experience what some book says is normal, free them to believe that "marriage is honourable in all and the bed undefiled." This freedom creates a climate for profitable mutual sharing between husband and wife.

While most men share the need for a wife, and while most women have the ability to meet the need of a man, each man and each woman is different. Each marriage then carries its own personality, its own stamp of divinity—one that God gives it. Why then should we be in bondage to what the novelist portrays and what the researchers dictate? Christian couples, wake up! God gave your marriage its own distinct mystery. Give yourself continually to comprehending it.

We write to encourage the young and old alike—see God as the designer of your marriage. He is the one who can always make a difference. Give Him His place in your marriage. Couples that walk with God and maintain a God-focus can be sure that their marriage will be all that God intends it to be. Someone has said, "Marriage takes three. Don't forget God."

1.

The Wonder

The Mystery of Love

Who can explain the love of Jesus? Who can understand the love that took Jesus through Gethsemane, through the scourgings of the judgment hall, and finally through the shame, the disgrace, and the curse of Calvary? Who can explain why men and women are willing to give up their lives in response to Christ's love? Christ's love is a mystery.

The Bible explains the love of Christ in these words: "Who for the joy that was set before him endured the cross, despising the shame, and is set down at the right hand of the throne of God" (Hebrews 12:2). Each Christian takes up his cross with the same vision. The cross always entails the surrender of self-interests. We take up the interests of another. But we see joy and glory coming after the cross. In our surrender we always gain more than we give. It is an inexplicable mystery that God wrapped up in the cross.

"Husbands, love your wives, even as Christ also loved the church, and gave himself for it" (Ephesians 5:25). Can a man love like Jesus? Where is the husband who can endure all that Christ endured? Christian husbands can and do have a measure of the love of Christ. It is a supernatural love. Every Christian marriage has this added dimension—the love of Christ. This joyous potential of the Christian marriage enables the husband to endure the cross to obtain the glorious end.

Who can explain the singularity of the love of a man preparing for marriage? The anticipation consumes most of his thoughts. Some young men become so engrossed with the thought of getting married that they can hardly keep their mind on their work. This preoccupation with expectation could be considered a fault. But is that not the way we are to anticipate the coming of the Bridegroom? Indeed marriage is a type of what we anticipate in our union with Jesus at His appearing.

Marriage Calls for Ceremony

Why do weddings attract so much attention? Why all the planning and fuss just to get two people married? Ah, friends, something as marvelous as marriage demands preparation, careful thought, and finally ceremony. Oh, the great marvel when the man takes the hand of his bride and God joins them together as husband and wife! While this couple is sure that their love is intense and full, they are only beginning to catch a little glimpse of a great mystery that will unfold with time if they keep God in their marriage.

If the new husband and wife know what it means to keep themselves in the love of God, they are about to experience unfolding glories unknown before. They will be like a budding astronomer looking into a powerful telescope for the first time. Suddenly before his eyes are galaxies he never saw before. Even the difficulties become part of the unfolding mystery—*if they do not forget the God who designed their marriage, if they view everything as controlled by Him.* Solomon's Song will then be their song.

Let me illustrate in a small way the importance of keeping God in view. Brother Daniel and his wife were returning to their home with their son and his wife after being refused entry at the Canadian border. They were on the interstate highway and would be passing Jonestown. There were gardens in that city that Daniel and his wife had once visited, and she suggested they visit them again. Brother Daniel had enjoyed visiting those manicured gardens, but not quite to the extent his wife had. Besides, he was still downhearted from being turned back at the border. He protested taking the time to visit the gardens.

His wife did not say much. They both knew he sometimes granted her wishes in spite of protesting at first. But on this particular occasion, he did not intend to stop.

But as Daniel was busy talking with his son, he suddenly realized he was leaving the interstate and entering a city. It was Jonestown! As he expressed his surprise over how this had happened, his wife said, "Oh, I thought you were taking us to see the gardens!"

Daniel said, "Well, dear, I'm sorry, but I can't take credit for that kind of thoughtfulness this time. But since we are here, we may as well see the gardens again." He added, "Isn't it marvelous how God seems to look out for the wife?"

Although they had accepted the refusal to enter Canada as God's will for them, the walk through the gardens was good therapy for them all. Those who keep God in focus can live without the buildup of tension on any matter. Oh, the mystery of love!

Brother Daniel mentioned that God seems to look out for the wife. He also looks out for the husband. Some wives are not as loving and considerate as they ought to be, and God intervenes for their husbands at times. When we continually look to God, He arranges the affairs of our marriage in a way that will best serve the union. How thankful we need to be that God cares for us all so tenderly when we fear Him. No wonder marriage calls for ceremony when we consider all that God is about to do.

The Sacrifice of Love

The sacrificial element of love adds to the mystery. When marital love is Christ's love, no suffering will be too great to endure for the beloved. This love is not centered on physical satisfaction between two people. It is a love that desires children to further extend the love bond. The ecstasies of the union will never rise to the highest possibilities if the couple focuses its love only on itself.

The true Christian maintains a Biblical view of family, with the desire for children being an integral part of it. A marriage love bond lacks something when there are no children, though God can fill that void. A degree of suffering and sacrifice accompanies this view, but the rewards outweigh the sacrifice if we follow God's directives. "Happy is the man that hath his quiver full of them" (Psalm 127:5).

The modern world's view of children goes, "Happy is the man who has the best number of children to serve his own purposes. One or two is about right." This kind of philosophy always leads to a sad end. Self-serving parents have self-serving children who abandon their parents in old people's homes all across the nation.

Unselfish marital love continually opens new vistas as time progresses. It has the potential to develop into an intense emotion that carries a couple through the storms and tempests that come to all. Every sacrifice becomes a joy as we maintain an intense interest in how we can make our companion the happiest. We all benefit by keeping the focus off ourselves.

Christ Gave Himself for the Church

Can you explain how Christ could completely surrender to death and in the end be the Lord of the church? How can He be both servant and Lord?

Can you explain how a Christian man can give himself for his wife and still be her leader? Few husbands think of themselves as servants to their wives. Yet Jesus became a servant, though He is Lord, and Christian husbands become servants too.

At times every nerve in our body cries out, "This is not fair! Father, let this cup pass from me." Yet love urges us on until we finally emerge on the bright side of the trial. When we marry we do not know to what extent our love will be tested. But, oh, the glory and peace we experience as we follow our Lord Jesus through every trial to victory.

Giving of ourselves for our wives involves everyday duties and routine courtesies. Christlike love urges us to do things we would not ordinarily do or things we would rather not do. But after we have passed the hardest tests, the little annoyances seem nothing. We even learn to enjoy whatever we do for our wife—be it changing the baby's diaper, mopping the floor Saturday evening, or washing the dishes Sunday noon.

By her very nature the wife is a servant to her husband and family. She must discover the joy of that service. Although her husband at times seems to take her service for granted, he really does appreciate her dedication to serving the union. Serving each other in marriage yields tremendous dividends.

Nourishing and Cherishing

The wise Christian husband does not let his marriage become ordinary or mundane. He maintains little interchanges with his wife that keep the caring relationship fresh. No one else needs to know anything about these private interchanges. They are mysteries. Others know that you love each other and they can tell that all is well between you, but no one really knows what makes it work. It is the mystery of marital love as God planned it.

The Song of Solomon is so expressive in its language that Christians are a little embarrassed to read it all in public. But Christian couples can learn much from it if they will. A husband especially can learn how to nourish and cherish his wife by privately giving verbal admiration of his wife's beauty. He should borrow language from Solomon if he has no words of his own.

One man said, probably as a joke, "I can live two months on a good compliment." No husband or wife should make his mate wait that long for a good compliment. In fact, if you are not in the habit of doing it every day, it probably will not happen at two-month intervals. Get in the habit early of seeing commendable things about your husband or wife, and say that you see them. For instance, when your wife arranges the meal artistically on the table, commend her for the beauty she has created. Thank her regularly for her promptness at mealtime, and for her skill in making the meal delicious.

To cherish means to treat with affection and tenderness—to keep fondly in mind. When a husband thinks fondly of his wife, he will treat her with tender affection. This tenderness is conveyed by his eyes, by the tone of his voice, by the gentle caresses and the private kisses he slips in along the way. Over the years, the cherishing husband maintains a "courtship" attitude that makes the marriage bond a powerful entity—one the devil cannot penetrate.

The Dynamics of Marital Love

When we consider the dynamics of marriage, we are thinking of its intensity, vigor, and force. The more intense the relationship, the greater will be its power in the life of the couple. This great, mysterious, powerful emotion is nothing less than the supernatural love of Christ. This is something no researcher can ever penetrate or understand. Praise God!

Marital love begins with the will. We will to love our companions under all circumstances. Because they fail to understand this, too many married couples worry about what they will do if love departs. The feeling of love might depart for a time, but the will to love is a matter of choice.

Having willed it, we seek out ways to translate our love into action. The more private and exclusive these actions are, the greater their value to the one we love. The privacy of our affections is indeed important. (Too often those who display affectionate conduct in public are not very affectionate in private. It is hypocrisy.) Affection is not only private but also very subtle. Although it may be done in the presence of others, only you and your mate know of the interchange. This is often done by the gleam that goes from eye to eye. Your mate soon detects acceptance and approval.

These little interchanges are invigorating. Few things can be more uplifting than to have one who is so closely involved in all that we do be so approving. This does not mean that we never disagree or disapprove of what our spouse has done, but it does mean that in any case we can communicate Christlike love, giving and accepting each other's encouragement.

Affection must wear work clothes to be truly effective. Husbands and wives want more than affectionate words. The interactions include working together in household duties, in gardening, in keeping order on the premises. The more we share in the everyday duties, the greater the bonding of the union. The mystery of Christ's love causes us to look for ways to do many things together.

If God is not at the center of the union, anything can go wrong. If Christ's love is not operating in the heart of the marriage, sensual love will often be deficient. Either partner may function in a way that will be hurtful if not destructive. We can keep God at the center only by seriously and sincerely seeking His will on all matters. Far too many couples enter marriage without knowing what it means to walk with God. Many couples cannot experience the dynamics of marriage because they have bypassed the Dynamo!

2.

The Plan

"An Help Meet for Him"

A husband said, "After I was married I was so happy to have a wife that was my very own possession." Depending how he felt about the things he possessed, his attitude could have been a great blessing to his wife, or it could have been a distress. The wife is indeed the husband's possession. The husband is also the wife's possession. The husband is rightfully protective and possessive of his wife. What we do and how we think about that possession makes a world of difference for both the husband and the wife.

It is no secret that many unhappy marriages do exist. Even among Christians some couples are not enjoying the blessings that God intended for them. Why is this? Did God hide the blessings from some and reveal them to others? Did God design marriage in a way that only a select few can discover the mystery? Is it God's plan that for some, marriage shall be a prison and for others a garden? Of course not. Then why do some marriages go wrong?

Basic to all good relationships is unselfishness. Marriage is no exception. Yet selfishness too often creeps in because marriage is designed by its very nature to supply a need in one's life. A man seeks a wife because it is not good for him to be alone. A wife accepts the proposal to marriage because of a natural desire in her own heart to be loved and cared for by a man. In the process of having their own needs met, they can be selfish. Natural, selfish motivation is a poor foundation for marriage. It will never lead to the mystery. True repentance must precede God's blessing.

A husband may rightfully be happy that he has exclusive right to his wife. But if he selfishly sets out to have his needs supplied and forgets that his wife has some needs also, then she is in a prison! On the other hand, if the husband is so happy to have this marvelous gift from God that he sets out to discover how he may best make her happy, then she is in a garden. The woman who marries simply to have a mate to satisfy her whims and desires is putting her husband in a prison. But if she marries because she believes this is God's will, she and her husband have some splendid opportunities to build a valuable relationship.

Possessed but Free

The idea of our mates being our possessions can give a wrong connotation. Wives, as well as husbands, can be possessive in a wrong way. Our mates remain individuals. As persons they have feelings, ideals, ideas, likes, and dislikes. Are our companions enjoying freedom or enduring bondage?

Some men seem to have the idea that, unless they make all the household decisions, they are not the head. This is one way for a man to make considerable inconvenience for himself. It will also frustrate his wife. Every couple must work out the details as to who is responsible for what. But the more freedom the husband can give to his wife, the greater will be her effectiveness in the marriage.

I allow my wife to manage the household. She decides what to buy for the house. Often she consults with me, but sometimes she does not. Sometimes I may question the wisdom of some purchase. That is turned around when it comes to business matters. I often counsel with her, and when I do not I too may be faced with some questions about the wisdom of a purchase. When Christ's love is reigning in the heart, this type of interchange is welcomed and even enjoyed.

Both husband and wife have spheres of responsibility. They are accountable to each other, yet they are free. Both may exercise themselves in the abilities that God has given them. These areas of responsibility may be different with each couple since everyone is different.

In one marriage the new wife was not used to handling money properly, and the husband shunned debt. He soon saw that something would need to be different. He kindly explained that he would do all the buying until patterns and understanding were developed. Their relationship developed into a successful marriage. Although she had some things to learn, she was the "help meet for him."

Of course there are men who do not seem to know how to manage their finances. Hopefully God will give them wives who do. Then if they are wise, they will see how kind God was and allow the wife to help them manage. But too often these men are already suffering from a sense of inferiority, and they suppose that to allow the wife to hold the purse is too humiliating. They seem to think that to delegate their responsibility to the wife or to take her advice amounts to surrender. The extent to which some men go to maintain what they consider their dignity is sad and shameful. Of course they always lose it when they try to save it. Oh that they would learn the mystery of being both the servant and the head.

Love Keeps Us Free

Every wife has tremendous potential to contribute to the marriage. But she cannot contribute that potential if she fears to expose her true self. It is true that "fear hath torment." It is also true that fear handicaps the fearful wife. It cheats her husband of all that she could have been.

The solution? "Perfect love casteth out fear" (1 John 4:18). A Christian husband wants a reciprocal love relationship where both are free from fears and doubts—a relationship where both are free to share their deepest sentiments.

As a husband ponders how well the helper God gave him is suited to him, he will discover that he has some needs that he had not even recognized. Responding properly to this requires humility. But it is also an opportunity, for a humble husband encourages the free flow of love. His respect for the counsel and concerns of his wife frees her from fear. As a free person, "she will do him good and not evil all the days of her life" (Proverbs 31:12).

Appreciating the Worst

The Christian husband should learn to give thanks even for those traits in his wife that another person would see as deficiencies. Why is this?

Every wife is a composite person. The husband promises to love and cherish her. He does this best by loving everything about her. Every trait she has distinguishes her from all others. There is no other person anywhere quite like her. Blessed is the man who learns to thank God for everything about his wife.

After all, in the marriage vows, does a man promise to love just the good traits of his wife? No indeed! He promises to love and cherish her as a complete person.

But should not the husband help his wife improve in those areas where she needs help? Certainly! And he should likewise let his wife help him with his weak spots. Let us put it this way. Both husbands and wives should love their spouses for their weaknesses as well as their strengths.

Someone made this observation. A husband, when he marries, thinks his wife is perfect, and he hopes she will always stay that way—but she does not. Time brings changes. The wife, when she marries, sees things in her husband that she hopes he will change with time—but he does not. He continues to do disappointing things even though she has reminded him of them.

How can a marriage survive under such disappointment? When we consider God's design in the matter, all comes together in this great mystery we call marriage. We do not need to know all that God has in mind for our marriage; we just need to follow His directions in the Bible and let Him work out the results.

How to Pass the Tests

Married life is a series of tests. One serious danger the husband faces is that of losing the God-focus. The husband who forgets that his wife is a gift from God will have many frustrations. He will begin to see his wife as a person who should be all that he expects. Some men, seemingly, are so self-centered that they expect their wives to be the first out of bed in the morning and the last to go to bed at night. They expect the house always to be clean even when there are three or four little ones to care for. They expect their meals always to be on time. They expect their wives to be perfect "like Mother always was!"

That, of course, is extreme. Hopefully no man is that

bad, but some come dangerously close to being that unreasonable. And of course they devastate their marriage. Some men expect more of their wives than they do of themselves or maybe even more than their wives are capable of doing. Such selfishness will not bring satisfaction to either husband or wife. Theirs will be an unhappy marriage.

God created the woman to be quite different from a man in her way of thinking about many things. Sometimes this baffles husbands. Many men are tempted to smile at their wives' thought patterns or, worse, to ridicule them. That is really sad, for her way of looking at a problem may be wiser than her husband's way. The Christian husband should be humble enough to understand this, acknowledge it, and use it to serve the marriage union. Too often a man begins to feel threatened by his wife's wise counsel, and he feels compelled to belittle her counsel or reason. This is very unfortunate for any marriage. It will destroy trust, respect, and love. It is pride, and God will fight against it.

If only men were wise enough—*and Christian enough*— to consider the special design and purpose of God's provision in the wife! The woman was not designed to think like a man. God made her very different from the man. She is a mystery to the man in many ways. The man has many things to learn about his wife. He cannot learn them all in one year or two and maybe not even in ten. A Christian man will pass the tests of marriage if he will continue to marvel and thank God for his wife, God's special provision.

Husbands who keep the God-focus are not chagrined,

dismayed, or distressed by the wife's feminine personality. They savor the mystery. They invariably worship and thank God for His infinite wisdom in providing a helper so perfectly designed for their good.

3.

The Wife

God Made a Woman

"And the rib, which the LORD God had taken from man, made he a woman, and brought her unto the man" (Genesis 2:22).

Let us consider further this woman whom God made. Woman is not a man with a few physical changes that distinguish her from the man. God made her a completely different person. He gave the woman characteristics so different that we call them feminine, while the man's characteristics are masculine. For instance, compare a typical woman's voice, gestures, and way of walking with a typical man's. Compare how they relate to little children, to teenage sons, to chimney fires, to crawl spaces. The differing masculine and feminine characteristics are designed to be complementary, not competitive.

The wise, God-fearing husband recognizes this early in his marriage. His interest in the feminine character grows rapidly as he discovers more and more the differences between himself and his wife. The husband who does not fear God sees the whole matter in a completely different light and is headed for frustration.

At the Fall of man, the marriage union suffered great loss. The experiences of many generations since the Fall should have taught people some lessons. But what have they learned? Little, because sin blinds man's eyes. Men and women enter into marriage without God—and then endure or divorce each other. Only a few couples discover the few simple rules that make a marriage work harmoniously. This is very unfortunate because God has a better way, and anyone who really seeks to understand God's purpose for marriage will be rewarded with a knowledge that blesses the union.

Today many in society hold erroneous ideas about women. One is that women are no different from men—that they can do anything a man can do in the labor market. This is not true. Women are indeed doing many things that in the past were left for men, but that does not prove that men and women are alike.

Women are resourceful. They can do marvelous things.

They can do things that a man cannot do. They can do some things with great dexterity that a man finds very awkward.

However, ungodly men have intimidated women for so long that now women are determined to do anything that a man can do. It is a shame to see all that women undertake, trying to prove that they are as capable as any man. What do they gain in the end? Maybe a few gain some admiration, but more often they gain the disrespect of those they are trying to impress.

Feminism a Misnomer

The "feminist movement" is a misnomer. You would think that it would be acting in the interest of women. It is not. It is another of Satan's ploys to destroy the work of God.

This movement destroys homes. Instead of helping women to find fulfillment and satisfaction in the feminine role as wives and mothers, the movement is designed to oppose the Biblical and traditional role for women. The painful thing about all this is that it is wasting the lives of many and causing great suffering and distress. This distress is not limited to women; it extends to children and to husbands.

The climate that this movement engenders in society will not allow anyone to discover the great mystery that God put into the marriage relationship. Any "Christian" who imbibes the feminists' teachings will suffer the same malady in his marriage as anyone else who implements their ideas. We must beware of their ideas ourselves.

Some couples have made some really notable efforts to function on the basis that no one is the head. They try to think in terms of complete equality between husband and wife. Some of these couples live this way for a while, but the setup can never endure because it is not according to God's plan. Couples who live like this must avoid having children because a child upsets the balance of things. They will not be able to give children proper attention.

Thankfully, for a few it seems that nature does take over and they have a child that changes their whole perspective. Various couples have testified of such a change. However, an unplanned-for child can cause resentments of which the poor child will be a victim. How gloriously different it is when a couple allows God to plan their life and their family!

Blessed Motherhood

God made the woman with special powers as a wife and mother. The world is a better place because of good wives and mothers. The wise woman will content herself in being one of those women.

God made the woman with natural abilities to care for infants and little children. He gave her a gentle touch and usually a soft voice that calms the fears of little ones. He even gave every natural mother hormones that affect her attitudes toward her children and enable her to be a good mother and wife. Adoptive mothers can, of course, make up the difference and love their adopted children as much as any natural mother loves her children. Women who take care of other people's children as a business cannot.

Modern daycare centers are a devastating tradeoff for the real mother. They are designed to accommodate the "working mother". (This title is a slap in the face of the homemaker, the *real* working mother!) Daycare centers are usually operated for a profit. As caring as their employees may want to be or profess to be, they cannot take the place of the real mother. Constant congregating of very small children will hinder normal development. No natural mother with a conscience can feel right about putting her child into this type of arrangement.

Blessed Homemaking

It is a terrible injustice to expect a woman to spend eight hours at a job and then try to fill the role of wife and mother. What is the purpose anyway? Sometimes it is to finance a lifestyle that does not satisfy. Sometimes it is to help the woman find fulfillment in a career outside the home, ignoring the fact that homemaking is in itself a career. Where did these ideas come from? Not from anyone who thinks clearly. The Bible speaks of people so persistent in sin that "God gave them over to a reprobate mind" (Romans 1:28). Maybe that casts some light on what is happening in today's society.

A woman in the workplace often gets the wrong kind of attention from men. This is bad for her marriage. So is the conflict that arises at home when her husband needs to help with the household duties. No wonder the husband is hard-pressed to think of commendable things to say to his wife. One result of all this is today's disastrously high divorce rate. How many marriages would be better with half the income if the wife were home, keeping the house in order?

How blessed is the husband who comes home to a meal prepared each day by the loving hand of his wife. How blessed the wife who hears every day the compliments and encouragement of her husband, rather than hearing other men in the workplace praise her.

Research Confirms Truth

We may question the wisdom of all the research being done on the differences between men and women, yet amazing things do come to light. For instance, scientists have learned that a man has ten times as much of the hormone testosterone as a woman does. At certain stages of life, the contrast is even greater than this. No doubt, in God's intricate design, there are many differences that the researchers have not discovered.

Christians cheerfully accept the fact that there is a difference between men and women. They learn to be impressed by the manifest wisdom of God in what He designed. We do not need the proofs of science to confirm our belief that God created the difference. The Christian husband and wife grow in their thankfulness for the way they can complement each other in life.

The extent to which some scientists go to try to prove that there is no difference is painful to consider. Men, women, and children all suffer when God's design is ignored or denied. This theory has contributed greatly to the many divorces that abound today. If there is no difference between men and women, then leadership in the home is a matter of debate and contest. This creates a conflict that usually ends in divorce. The poor, benighted couple never discovers that there is a great mystery to marriage—a mystery that God designed to absorb and enthrall the married couple.

Do Not Forget God

The whole purpose of life is altered when men forget God. Their supposedly wise ideas always lead to disaster. "Because that, when they knew God, they glorified him not as God, neither were thankful; but became vain in their imaginations, and their foolish heart was darkened. Professing themselves to be wise, they became fools" (Romans 1:21, 22). Some people are beginning to see that divorce is taking a great toll on society. They are beginning to think of ways to reverse the trend. The only real solution is to turn back to God and recognize the vital role that God's design plays in the marriage of one man to one woman.

4.

The Husband

The Man Needs Help

"And the LORD God said, It is not good that the man should be alone; I will make him an help meet for him" (Genesis 2:18).

Some men never marry. Jesus said that there are various reasons why this may be (Matthew 19:12). The apostle Paul gave his opinion about people remaining unmarried in order to serve the Lord without distraction. See 1 Corinthians 7. He did concede that every man has his proper gift.

Marriage is indeed a gift. Every Christian husband

should thank God for the gift of marriage. We cannot do this unless we are enjoying our marriage. We cannot enjoy our marriage unless we conduct ourselves according to God's plan for us.

Salvation Comes First

God created man with a need for a wife. Then man fell from his sinless state, and he now has an even greater need—he needs Jesus. He needs to be saved.

Since man is a sinner, the normal physical needs are points of temptation. The need for food is perverted into a craving for excessive indulgence in food. Of course it is not wrong to enjoy food. A Christian learns to enjoy many simple foods. But needing to indulge in delicacies is an earmark of the inordinate desires of a carnal heart.

For example, Israel was receiving manna in the wilderness. This special food contained all that the body needed. But the people fell to lusting. They did not use moderation when God gave them meat. God slew many of them because of their lusting.

Man's need for a wife is also subject to abuse. The normal desire for companionship has been perverted. Rather than marrying in order to share life with a wife, man uses his wife to satisfy his lusts. This is sin. Few ungodly men ever learn the value and intensity of focused love. When sensual pleasures wane with their mate, they go lusting after another.

God expects us to control our appetite when we sit down

to a table full of food. Many times people sin when they eat more than they need. The same is true in relation to our need for sleep. Some sleep too much. They are sinfully lazy. Likewise, man needs to work. Some work too much and do not rest enough. This also is sin. The same applies to husband and wife relationships. The Christian husband must not think only of satisfying his own desires. He must try to satisfy his wife. Ephesians 5 outlines clearly how a Christian husband will love his wife as Christ loved the church. The spiritual husband desires to see his wife find fulfillment in her role as much as he wants to find fulfillment in his.

God designed marriage to be reciprocal. When the husband becomes a leader in self-denial, likely his wife will also deny herself, and the union will be glorious. Let the husband or the wife inject some selfishness, and the glory will dissipate rapidly.

Man needs a Saviour to deliver him from his lusts. He needs a Lord to be his guide and master, and he needs the grace of God. Sometimes a young man is troubled with desires that cannot rightly be fulfilled outside of marriage. He must first of all commune with God and allow Jesus to control his life. Until he has done this, the man is not ready to put the wife first in his life. He must first develop a focused love—a love for God. He must ask God to teach Him what focused love is. The more focused love is, the greater its value to the one who does the loving.

Machismo does not characterize the Christian husband. That is a development of devil-controlled men. Rather than

43

asserting our manliness, we seek to be like Jesus. The Christian husband does not glory because he is the leader of the union. He is humbled to consider that a woman has chosen to come under his care and direction. He prays continually for wisdom to know how to properly care for this helper God gave him.

The husband who feels compelled to assert his manliness or who continually reminds his wife that he is the head is acting like a spoiled child. His satisfaction is juvenile and perverse in that it comes at the expense of another. He is acting out of fear rather than love. It may be a matter of ignorance, but it is foolish conduct nonetheless. This is tragic because in such a frame of mind, he can never begin to enjoy a marriage as God designed it. He should take careful stock of his relationship with the Lord, or begin one. He will discover that putting that relationship first solves many of his problems.

5.

The Union

The Mystery of the Union

"They two shall be one flesh" (Ephesians 5:31). "What therefore God hath joined together, let not man put asunder" (Matthew 19:6). God joins husband and wife together for life. The couple who believes this and takes it seriously can embark on a journey together with reproductive potential. God usually gives them the ability to bring immortal souls into this world.

To fearful, timid souls, this is scary. To the God-fearing couple, it is a welcome opportunity. Godly couples want children. In Bible times, barrenness was considered a curse. Today we still consider children in the home a great blessing. We generally encourage childless couples to adopt children.

If properly nurtured and satisfied, sexual desire is at least in part the glue of the union. Every married couple has things to learn about this that go beyond finding self-ish fulfillment. Peter instructs husbands to dwell with wives according to knowledge (1 Peter 3:7). The husband gains that knowledge through communication with his wife.

One evening as a Christian brother was preparing for the night, he discovered a book lying on his pillow. He looked up to see his wife smiling as tears ran down her cheeks. She said, "You should have bought that book for yourself." The title was *What Every Wife Wishes Her Husband Knew.* He knew then that he had some things to learn. They had been married too many years not to know some of the things he needed to know. He read the book and tried to learn all he could from it. It was beneficial because no one had taught him how to conduct himself as a husband.

Husbands do not naturally know everything they need to know about their wives. They know they need wives, and they have natural desires that lead them to marriage. But they do not know much about the feminine character-istics that make the wife the good companion she is. God wrapped up a good supply of mystery in both the mascu-line and the feminine character. In marriage we enter into those mysteries and discover them together.

Fathers can equip their sons with some introductions to this knowledge. Bishops can share some basics with the newly weds. Husband, you should know that your wife normally has the capacity to enjoy the physical union as much as you do. It is your responsibility to learn from her what gives her pleasure. Communicate with her and *take the needed time* to discover the mysteries of the feminine response. Be aware of her varying moods and be considerate.

When we love like Christ, we put our wife's joys and pleasures ahead of ours. We do so consistently, remembering that marriage is a twenty-four-hour-a-day proposition. We do things for our wives throughout the day that convey love and consideration.

The wife should be patient and understanding. She needs to rightly interpret her husband's love. She should realize how valuable she is to her husband. He needs a wife who understands something about his needs. She must understand what temptations he faces when he does not receive "due benevolence" (1 Corinthians 7:3). Her unresponsiveness to him is especially frustrating if he is doing his best to make her happy.

A wife benefits when her husband is enjoying his marriage relationship. Wife, if you feel cheated or used, talk to God about it. Ask Him to give you wisdom to know how to develop understanding between you and your husband. Choose a time when there is no tension and discuss the matter. Seek help from your mother or father or a minister's wife if you need further help.

The subject is delicate and difficult to talk about, but it is right and proper to do so when necessary. God wrapped up tremendous powers and possibilities in the marriage union. It is an unfolding experience that includes more and more involvements as time moves on—even the propagation of new life. We realize its greatest potential as we abandon all selfishness and practice "due benevolence" one to another.

The Potential of the Union

The young Christian couple who look into the face of their newborn child are awed by what God has given them. The months of preparation and waiting have set their focus on something other than themselves. God's great law comes into focus—"Whosoever will save his life shall lose it: and whosoever will lose his life for my sake shall find it" (Matthew 16:25).

The world does not view the child as a gift from God. We hear of some Christian couples who intentionally delay the arrival of children to the union. As a rule, this is selfish. Sometimes after they decide to have children, they discover that God has deemed them unworthy

Children are a blessing to the Christian home. Their entrance adds to the mystery and multiplies the pleasures. Children call for more sacrifice, and the more we learn the value of sacrifice, the greater our pleasures. Oh, the mysteries of God.

Childhood candor alone blesses Christian parents. They are completely free from hypocrisy. They innocently expose their parents. Once a man changed his mind about something and used the proverb his mother had often used. "A wise man changes his mind, and a fool never does." His little son innocently raised his eyebrows and said, *"Wise* man?" Sometimes fathers need to be humbled. Are we as wise as we think we are?

One great benefit parents receive from children is the humiliation that accompanies child training at times. Someone made this observation: Children as they are growing up embarrass their parents; later the parents embarrass their teenage children. It all serves God's purposes quite well.

The Gospels show us Jesus' lofty view of children. The disciples thought that a man so important as Jesus should not be bothered with children. But He took them up in His arms and blessed them. The children's song puts it perfectly—"Jesus loves the little children, all the children of the world." "Happy is the man that hath his quiver full of them" (Psalm 127:5). Christian marriages are indeed greatly blessed when God gives them children.

The Comfort of the Union

The marriage union is not only for procreation. Marriage is the sharing of every experience possible. We always want our mates to be happy. They share everything intimately—the mutual joys, sorrows, pains, and pleasures. Couples that learn to communicate intimately on every level in every experience will enjoy marriage as God intended. Indeed, one can endure some very mean treatment if he knows that he has an understanding companion.

Many are the times when I can hardly wait to get with

my wife to share some news or happening. I come home with a bit of expectation that she might have something to share with me. She is an avid reader and often shares with me what she reads. We anticipate sharing not only our joys but also our sorrows.

This world is not always a friendly place. In fact, it can be quite hostile. If the marriage relationship is not good, the husband might come home to further hostilities, or the wife may dread the return of her husband. Constant conflict finally causes emotional disorders.

What can be done about this? In the world, couples divorce; but among Christians this is not an option. On rare occasions, they might separate for a time, but this often causes further frustration.

How much better it is when a couple maintains a holy union! They can always come home to a place of comfort. God designed marriage to be just that—a place of rest and peace.

Naomi said to her widowed daughter-in-law, "Shall I not seek rest for thee, that it may be well with thee?" (Ruth 3:1). Marriage brings rest when the union functions properly. Inject selfishness at any point, and the union is threatened. The threat is always removed when there is forgiveness. But if selfishness is not confronted and repented of, the marriage will become dysfunctional. Instead of rest, there will be turmoil. Instead of anticipation, there will be revulsion. Instead of excitement, there will be endurance. How sad to allow something with such joyous potential to fail to reach its God-given design!

Input Determines Outcome

Part of the mystery of the marriage union is this paradox: the more one puts into the relationship, the more he gets from it. Persons who feel they are not getting out of marriage all they need, usually need to put more into it. That way they have an emotional bank account from which to draw.

The more selfless we are, the greater will be our rest and peace. This is true of both husband and wife. It is often my selfishness that makes me see my wife's selfishness. If a husband willingly sacrifices himself to please his wife she will likely give herself in greater self-sacrifice too. Since the husband is the leader of the union, he should take the lead in sacrificing self. But the wife, because of her nature, is often the one who makes the greater sacrifice. The husband needs to put forth more effort to be like Jesus in sacrifice. It is difficult, but it is rewarding. It is one of those rewards hidden in the mystery.

Selfish conduct is continually a possibility. For that reason I must daily deny self, take up my cross, and follow Jesus. I did not become naturally unselfish after ten years of marriage. Selfishness remains a temptation even after forty years. The same is true of my wife. Any situation can create a conflict if we disagree. But we have learned to blend our thinking on all matters. We have learned the value of mutual consideration.

To do this, we continually draw from God's fountain of grace. When we forget God, we fail and sin. God allows us to be chastised, and then we repent. With true repentance the blessings continue.

Marriage Sanctifies the Union

As you consider the mystery of the union, think about this. How can a physical union between a man and woman be so sinful outside of marriage and yet so completely right and proper within it?

The potential that God put into the union is one reason for this. While God can and does control conception, He does not free people from the consequences of sinful behavior. Children born out of wedlock are deprived of many blessings that God planned for them. These children never experience parental love as it should be in marriage. They seldom develop properly when they are deprived of the opportunity to express filial love.

This is serious because immortal souls are involved. It is also serious because a society becomes unstable if many children are reared in homes without filial love. For these reasons, and more, sexual intercourse outside of marriage is sinful—so sinful in fact that adultery was punishable by death under the Mosaic Law. There is nothing right about it—no justification for it. It is sin.

Reciprocation of the Union

In Solomon's Song we often have difficulty discerning where the bridegroom stops talking and the bride takes up the strains of love and admiration. This is as it should be. The one is not always giving and the other receiving; each one contributes, and each receives. What each one contributes is not the same. The masculine contribution is different from the feminine. The wife cannot provide what the husband needs to contribute. Each must give his part.

This reciprocation is different for each couple because each person has individual weaknesses and needs that the other supplies. It is marvelous to see these variations working together smoothly when couples love the Lord. People who are very different from each other form a union that succeeds.

The sharing of marriage is simply beautiful when you see those couples who have learned to abandon themselves to the union. They weather the storms together without accusing one another. They rejoice together in their successes. They have the light of heaven in their eye as they go about daily tasks.

It is sad to see those who simply endure their marriage because they have not learned to respect each other. Is it not one of the mysteries of life how one can be so close to real blessing and yet never discover it? The secret is surrender to God and to our companion. Once we have learned that, the blessings will flow.

The Mystery of Submission and Reverence

"Therefore as the church is subject unto Christ, so let the wives be to their own husbands in every thing.... And the wife see that she reverence her husband" (Ephesians 5:24, 33). These verses sum up the duties of the wife. On the surface this sounds risky—and it is. But the mystery of love makes this mystery follow in natural sequence.

Where the man subjects himself completely to Christ, loves his wife as Christ loves the church, and nourishes and cherishes her, the wife will gladly submit herself to him in everything and even reverence him. But man is not perfect in his submission to Christ. He is not perfectly Christlike in his love. He is negligent sometimes in the nourishing and cherishing aspects of his duty. He is a human and fails sometimes. This puts a real test to the wife.

Will the wife obey God and submit and reverence this failing man? Will she forgive him and fulfill her duty if the husband fails in his? Herein lies the mystery of submission and reverence. If the wife becomes resentful, her peace and power are gone. But if she remains faithful, she has great potential to help her husband. If she fulfills her part even though her husband is not the perfect man she desires him to be, she will have God's blessing and peace.

Likewise, a husband's peace is not dependent on a completely submissive wife. In fact, a wife who is submissive in everything is probably as rare as a husband who always loves his wife as Christ loved the church. Yet each time we yield ourselves to Christ in full obedience, we have the peace and power we desire.

The more completely we abandon ourselves to fulfilling our part of the marriage commitment, the greater will be the blessings of the union. God supplies the grace needed to repent when we fail. Although this is difficult, it always puts us on the path of blessing. New "galaxies" of the mystery appear before our eyes as we walk with the Lord in our marriage.

Some husbands have become very perturbed because their wives were not subject to them on some matter or other. Yet those men usually failed to love as Christ loved. When husbands concern themselves with being faithful in their part, and wives focus on their part, marriages do work as God planned. But if one spouse focuses on the failure of the other, that couple is in trouble.

This is all contrary to what we think naturally. We think our peace and happiness depends on how our mate treats us. No doubt our mate can make life miserable for us if we allow them to. But if we keep our mind stayed on God, we have perfect peace.

This is one of the paradoxes of godliness. We continually need God's grace to not allow others' responses to detract us from obeying God. The wife can submit in everything even if her husband does not love her as Christ loved the church. The husband can love his wife as Christ loved the church even if she is not subject to him in everything. This brings peace.

There is a strong possibility that if one is faithfully doing his part, the other will respond and come much closer to fulfilling the counterpart as well. On the other hand, if one fails and the other resents it, the downhill spiral begins. Turning around such a spiral may require some outside help.

The blessings associated with complete submission and reverence can never be realized until we practice complete submission and reverence. There is no other way for the wife to experience the dynamics of love. She may enjoy some marital pleasures, but she can never experience the fullness of God's peace and power until she offers all. If she carries any reservations, the door to the holy mystery will be closed. When she yields up every reserve, the door will swing open and the blessings will flow out.

This yielding is probably the most difficult thing a wife must do. It parallels the husband's need to love as Christ loved. The yielding, as well as the loving, calls for complete surrender to God. This brings us back to the God-focus. Jesus called it taking up our cross. It is a dying to self and taking up an interest contrary to self. It is rising above the tendency of the flesh when it says, "But I don't want to do that."

The husband must surrender his self-love in order to love as Christ loved. The wife must surrender her self-love to submit to her husband in everything. The demand is the same for both husband and wife, and the full reward is locked behind the same door. Ah, the mystery and its discovery!

6.

The Complexity

The Chemistry of Marriage

It is fitting for a Christian to think about the chemistry of marriage. We are not thinking about the chemistry of science but rather "the elements of a complex entity and their dynamic interrelation" *(American Heritage College Dictionary)*. The blood that flows in our veins is a complex entity. Its work is carried on with a dynamic interrelation with the parts of the body. Our emotions we experience affect the activity of our blood—whether hatred or love, excitement or calm.

The complex entity in marriage is the union of a man with a woman. Their dynamic interrelation is complex because it involves emotions and attitudes, looks and words, actions and motives, and almost everything about them.

The love we first felt for the one we married created excitement. While the excitement of love takes on different dimensions in the marriage relationship, it can be maintained. Couples can keep alive the romance of marriage, or they can let it die. We can keep romance surface-oriented, or we can allow it to gain depth and penetrate far beyond the flowers and the cards and the sweet talk.

I am not saying that a time comes when the husband no longer needs to buy flowers or give a card or say sweet things to his wife. But the husband who buys flowers out of duty is probably failing to cultivate a relationship at a deeper level. Perhaps he is allowing the relationship to deteriorate and then trying to keep it patched up with gifts or sweet talk. Nothing can take the place of a continual interest in and attention to the things that matter to your mate. How many wives could say, "I don't want your flowers; I want you"?

The Communication

Marriage is a union so intertwined that each comes to know what the other would think or do in any situation. This kind of personal knowledge of the other may require several years to develop, depending on the amount of communicating a couple does. Taking time to communicate has

value in itself. Even when a spouse knows what tl.
will say, he can sometimes "buy time" or delay a per.
decision by saying, "I will talk this over with my spous

A young sister once angered a telemarketer when sh.
said, "I will want to talk this over with my husband first."
The marketer was indignant. "You mean that you have to
talk everything over with your husband?" The sister said,
"No I don't have to. I want to!" Really, we can feel sorry
for those who have never discovered the great blessings of
the truly shared life.

We wrote earlier about the many secret signals that can
pass between a couple even while they are in the company
of others. Hopefully every signal is one of love. Disgust,
rejection, acceptance, or approval will be communicated
in various ways. Oh, the great privilege to always sense
the approval of your mate! If for some reason we err and
our companion needs to withhold approval, we should be
quick to repent in order to maintain a basic approval and
acceptance.

These wholesome attitudes make a difference in the
health of the body as well as of the soul. A heart that is free
from all bitterness and resentment also helps the blood-
stream to be free of destructive elements. Happily married
couples who are blissfully carrying on a continual, recip-
rocating exchange, often enjoy good health.

But if an individual feels rejection or feels inadequate
to please his mate, he will experience stress that will further hinder his effectiveness. Stress saps an enormous
amount of energy. With depleted energy the body is more

͟ble to disease. Every married couple should con-
͟ly guard against doing anything that causes bitter-
͟s or resentment to enter the marriage.

Since marriage involves two people with different view-
points, disagreement is always a possibility. In any conflict, someone must give in. God, foreseeing this, established
the husband as the head of the wife. The husband must be
satisfied in his heart that he is doing what is right. A Christian husband will not lead in such a way that the wife cannot be at rest in her heart also. She must be convinced in
her heart that God is pleased with what they do in their
marriage. This is very important in maintaining a beauti-
fully satisfying union. It is all a part of the intricate design
that God planned. It provides checks and balances for both
husband and wife in their Christian walk.

7.

The Secret

Even though we all move about in public, marriage is largely private. No one but the married couple knows what all goes on between them. It should not need to be anyone else's business unless there are serious difficulties. While children in a home observe more about the marriage than most observers do, there is still a private aspect that not even the children know anything about.

We can call this private aspect of marriage the inner sanctum. Usually the secrets of this sanctum are shared in the bedroom. Here many private discussions are conducted. Here husband and wife can open their hearts to one another. Here affections are freely shared. Here conflicting opinions e blended and problems resolved. And here hurts are healed as apologies are made and forgiveness is freely granted. Couples should not allow any fear to enter this chamber except godly fear.

Private conflicts should be resolved as quickly as possible. Make a sensible analysis. What is causing the conflict? What part does selfishness have in it? What parts do truth and error have in it? Is the issue so important that it should threaten marital harmony? What compromise can be made? Can it be safely tabled for further consideration at another date? Think of ways to be conciliatory.

The wise Christian couple will learn how to make this inner sanctum the citadel of their marriage—the place where the real glue of love and affection is applied to the union. They may want to make some rules as to what will be allowed to enter. Maybe they will decide that no conflicts will be allowed in that room. They may decide that only positive subjects will be discussed there. At any rate, each couple should understand the value of keeping the inner sanctum holy and beneficial to the union. In this place marriages are made or destroyed.

Privacy adds glory to the mystery. Even the Bible discreetly passes over some details of marriage; Proverbs 5:15–21 uses figurative language. The word *ravished* as used in "Be thou ravished always with her love" is worthy of notice and study.

God also masterfully included Solomon's Song in His Word to man. It can be properly used as a manual for marriage. It teaches marriage partners how to verbalize affection in private and what to see and comment on to their mates. Solomon again used the word *ravished* in 4:9. This song helps to keep alive the "ravishing" aspect of the marriage union. Older husbands especially should continually reassure their wives of how attractive they are. Love can grow to such a powerful state that everything about one's loved one is beauty and glory. Where this love abounds, security is at its zenith. Let others think or say what they will, this couple will be content and secure in God's love.

The mystery of marriage is God—the Infinite One who writes infinity into every union. Each couple joined in marriage is a unique entity. There is not another marriage anywhere like it. God joins it, watches over it, gives it its own joys and sorrows, hides within its confines the possibilities of ecstasy holy and sacred, builds into it checks and balances that enable one to experience peace in the midst of woe, and ties a knot so tight that only death can rightfully break it.

8.

Heirs Together

"Likewise, ye husbands, dwell with them according to knowledge, giving honour unto the wife, as unto the weaker vessel, and as being heirs together of the grace of life; that your prayers be not hindered" (1 Peter 3:7).

Life is for living—a living that is enjoyable and satisfying. God has this in His plan for each man and each woman. When two are united in marriage, they are prime candidates for enjoyment and satisfaction because they are "heirs *together* of the grace of life." After marriage everything relevant to the marriage can be shared and should be shared.

Many couples never quite come to experience this sharing to its full capacity. For some, pride is a limiting factor.

They barely admit their temptations and weaknesses to themselves, let alone to anyone else. For others, fear keeps them from the perfect love that would allow them to be free to communicate. "If you really knew me," they think, "you might not love me." Still others are simply ignorant of how to implement God's plan.

It takes time to learn what the limiting factors are in a particular marriage—whether pride, fear, or ignorance. Individuals vary greatly. Some are very forward and bold, while others are quiet and reserved. But the personality of an individual is not the most important thing. Rather, it is the focus of the couple. Those who focus only on themselves and on ways to fix their own problems will pine in frustration, but those who keep focused on God will discover His plan and glory in the marriage union.

Peter was writing to Christians. They inherit things in this life that the ungodly never do. Christian husbands and wives have resources in God that enable them to live life to its fullest potential. God gives them strength to endure experiences that cause others to despair. God gives them wisdom and understanding in matters that baffle the sinner. God gives them a love that carries them through trials and afflictions. This strength, wisdom, and love is combined and shared. Its fullest potential is realized as husband and wife blend their abilities.

Peter directs the husband to give "honour unto the wife, as unto the weaker vessel." The feminine physique is generally weaker than the masculine. Even though some robust women marry frail men, every man is commanded ᴑ treat his wife with honor.

"Giving honour unto the wife" is said in the context of being heirs together of life's grace. Honor, as well as dishonor, has many forms. Yet every Christian husband knows whether his conduct toward his wife is honorable or not.

Every wife has the right to enjoy life. No man has the right to make marriage a bondage for his wife. Of course no wife has the right to make marriage a bondage for her husband. True, we call marriage wedlock, but not because marriage is a prison. Marriage is wedlock because it is secure. Certainly it is secure for Christians, and that security adds value and pleasure. Solomon wrote it this way: "A garden inclosed is my sister, my spouse; a spring shut up, a fountain sealed" (Song of Solomon 4:12). Later he spoke of a "fountain of gardens, a well of living waters, and streams from Lebanon." Solomon's Song is full of the "grace of life" lived to its fullest. Indeed, marriage is a type of our union with Jesus. It is vibrant. It is alive with God's abundant grace for both husbands and wives.

Husband, are you doing all you can to make your wife's life enjoyable? Look at her face. Is it radiant with love and peace? Or is it lined with care and distress? Can she freely share her feelings on all matters without fearing ridicule? Can she count on you for help and support and understanding? Your wife is an heir of the grace of life along with you.

Wife, are you doing all within your power to make your husband a happy man? Look at his face. Is it radiant with peace and contentment? Are you helping him to stay focused on God? Is he able to be the leader of your marriage? Can he feel confident of your love and respect? Your husband is an heir of the grace of life along with you. Although you may be the weaker one, do contribute your God-given strength to make the union all God desires it to be.

When Christian couples live together with God's grace upon them, they can pray effectively. They know that nothing can hinder their spiritual life more than poor communications in the marriage. When they freely share all matters and are together in their prayer concerns, they find spiritual power to face anything.

"What is your life? It is even a vapour that appeareth for a little time, and then vanisheth away" (James 4:14). How then can you live life to its fullest? Give it to God. Allow Him to sanctify it and bless it, and then whatever state you are in will be a blessing.

"Marriage takes three. Don't forget God!"

> One thought I have, my ample creed,
>   So deep it is and broad,
> And equal to my every need—
>   It is the thought of God.
>
> Each morn unfolds some fresh surprise;
>   I feast at life's full board,
> And rising in my inner skies
>   Shines forth the thought of God.

The Mystery of Marriage

At night my gladness is my prayer;
    I drop my daily load,
And every care is pillowed there
    Upon the thought of God.

I ask not far before to see,
    But take in trust my road;
Life, death, and immortality
    Are in my thought of God.

Be still the light upon my way,
    My pilgrim staff and rod,
My rest by night, my strength by day—
    O blessed thought of God.

                —*Frederick L. Hosmer, 1880*